12 ARTISTS
WITH DISABILITIES

by Susan Perry

STORY LIBRARY

MORE TO EXPLORE

www.12StoryLibrary.com

12-Story Library is an imprint of Bookstaves.

Photographs ©: Kyodo/Associated Press, cover, 1; Lorenzo Dalberto/Alamy, 4; Skavlan/YouTube, 5; 20m2/YouTube, 6; HuffPost/YouTube, 7; Mlliu2006/CC4.0, 8; Kyodo/Associated Press, 9; JaviiVlogs/YouTube, 10; JaviiVlogs/YouTube, 11; PD, 11; Gina Ferazzi/Getty Images, 12; VCG/Getty Images, 14; PD, 15-17; PopTech/CC2.0, 18; PopTech/CC2.0, 19; Edward Weston/CC2.0, 20; Carl Van Vechten/Library of Congress, 21; Magda Pach/PD, 21; RJ Muna/World Arts West, 22; Richard Dowing/Sins Invalid, 23; Wig Worland/Alamy, 24; QuentinUK/CC3.0, 25; BrillLyle/CC4.0, 26; PD, 27; belushi/Shutterstock.com, 28; Africa Studio/Shutterstock.com, 29; J. McPhail/Shutterstock.com, 29

ISBN
9781632357519 (hardcover)
9781632358608 (paperback)
9781645820352 (ebook)

Library of Congress Control Number: 2019938643

Printed in the United States of America
October 2019

About the Cover

Nobuyuki Tsujii in concert in Tokyo, Japan, in 2017.

Access free, up-to-date content on this topic plus a full digital version of this book. Scan the QR code on page 31 or use your school's login at 12StoryLibrary.com.

Table of Contents

Evelyn Glennie: Keeping the Beat

While growing up on a farm in Scotland, Evelyn Glennie loved to play the piano and clarinet. She wanted to be a musician. But when she was eight years old, her ears started to hurt. Her parents took her to a doctor. She was told she had a rare medical condition that would cause her to lose her hearing.

By her twelfth birthday, Glennie was deaf. She could hear only a few sounds. Most of the ones she heard, like people's voices, sounded muddled.

Glennie was very angry. She still wanted to be a musician. But how could she become one when she couldn't hear?

Glennie playing percussion in 2015.

Her school music teacher showed her how. He taught her how to play a large timpani drum. He then explained how the drum's vibrations could help her "hear" music. Glennie discovered that she could feel low sounds in her feet and high sounds in her face, neck, and chest.

Glennie grew up to become a percussionist—a musician who plays drums and other instruments that can be struck, scraped, or shaken. She has played with orchestras and other musical groups around the world. She usually performs barefoot so she can feel the music's vibrations in her feet.

Many composers have written special music for Glennie. In 1988, she received a Grammy award for one of her records. It is one of the top awards a musician can get.

1,300
Percussion instruments Evelyn Glennie owns

- One instrument, a botanka, is made from plastic drainage pipes.
- Glennie invented it herself.
- A composer wrote special music for Glennie to play on the botanka.

THINK ABOUT IT

Sounds and vibrations are both "heard" in the same part of the brain. Do you ever notice vibrations when you're listening to music?

Mariusz Kedzierski: Expressing Himself Through Drawing

Mariusz Kedzierski in 2017.

holds the pencil against the ends of his arms.

Drawing became Kedzierski's favorite thing to do. But he had to stop drawing when he was 12 years old for health reasons. Then, in 2008, he had a surgical operation that made it possible for him to hold a pencil again. He's been drawing ever since.

Kedzierski likes drawing portraits, or pictures of people, the best. He says he is able to express his own feelings in his sketches of other people's faces. His portraits are incredibly realistic. They look just like the people he is drawing. Each drawing takes him about 20 hours to finish.

Kedzierski's drawings have been shown in art galleries around the world. He has also won many awards for them.

Mariusz Kedzierski was born without hands in Poland in 1992. His left arm ends just below his shoulder, and his right arm ends just below his elbow. Despite not having hands, Kedzierski started drawing pictures when he was three years old. He

17

Days it took Mariusz Kedzierski to complete his "Mariusz Draws" project in 2015

- Kedzierski traveled to nine cities in Europe, including London, Paris, and Rome.
- He sat outdoors in those cities and drew portraits of people he met on the streets.
- He wanted to inspire everyone to think about what they can do rather than what they can't do.

A FOCUS ON THE FACE

A portrait is a work of art that focuses on the face. It can be a drawing, a painting, a sculpture, or even a photograph. A traditional portrait shows a person's head and shoulders. But portraits can show a person's entire body, too. Portraits sometimes include more than one person. Many artists do self-portraits that feature their own faces. Artists also make portraits of pets and other animals.

Nobuyuki Tsujii: Playing for Gold

In 2009, 20-year-old Nobuyuki Tsujii won the top prize—a gold medal—at the Van Cliburn International Piano Competition. It is one of the most famous piano competitions in the world.

Tsujii was the first person from Japan to win a gold medal at that competition. He was also the first person who is blind to win it. He has been blind all his life.

Tsujii uses Braille to learn his piano pieces. In Braille, musical notes are represented by raised dots. People read the dots by moving their fingers across them.

Only a few pieces of music have been written in Braille. So Tsujii has created another way of learning new music. He has helpers who make audio recordings of small sections of

each piece. Tsujii listens to these sections over and over again until he has all the musical notes

Nobuyuki Tsujii in 2015.

memorized. He calls these recordings "music sheets for the ear."

Nobuyuki Tsujii in concert in Tokyo, Japan, in 2017.

Tsujii has become one of Japan's best-known musicians. He plays the piano in concert halls around the world. He also composes music. He has written several theme songs for Japanese movies.

4

Nobuyuki Tsujii's age when he started taking piano lessons

- Tsujii won his first piano competition when he was 7.
- He had his first concert with a major orchestra when he was 10.
- He started composing music when he was 12.

PERFECT PITCH

Tsujii has a special ability called perfect pitch. It means he can hear a sound and immediately know what note (or pitch) that sound is on a musical scale. It also means that if you were to ask Tsujii to sing an F-sharp note, he could do it right away. He wouldn't have to hear it first. Not all people who are blind have perfect pitch. And many people who aren't blind have it.

4

Christy Brown: Finding a Way to Tell His Story

1962

Christy Brown in 1962.

12 brothers and sisters. Doctors told his parents that he should be sent to live in an institution for the disabled, far from his home. But Brown's mother wouldn't let the doctors take him. She was worried he wouldn't live very long at the institution. She wanted to care for him herself.

Christy Brown was born in Dublin, Ireland, in 1932. He had a severe form of cerebral palsy. This is a condition that affects the body's muscles. Brown couldn't control his arms or legs—except the toes on his left foot. Because he couldn't walk, he had to be carried or pushed around in a wheelchair. Because he couldn't move his hands, he had to be fed by someone else.

Brown's family was very poor. It was also large. He had

22

Christy Brown's age when he published his first book

- It was an autobiography —a book about his life.
- Brown called it *My Left Foot*.
- It was made into an award-winning movie in 1989.

Brown's book, *My Left Foot*, was published in 1954.

So Brown stayed with his family. He got to play every day with his brothers and sisters. They included him in all their activities. They would put him in a wheelbarrow and take him around Dublin to their sports games or parties. Brown didn't attend much school, but his mother taught him how to read. She also taught him how to grasp chalk and a paintbrush with the toes on his left foot. That made it possible for him to write and draw.

Brown became a well-known writer and painter. He often wrote and painted about what he knew best— the things he heard and saw growing up in a poor but loving family in Dublin. Brown died in Ireland in 1981.

Laurie Rubin: Singing Around the World

Laurie Rubin performs in 2012.

Laurie Rubin started taking piano lessons when she was four years old. She loved music. But she didn't like to practice the piano. She preferred to sing the notes rather than play them on the piano.

When Rubin was 11 years old, she went to a performance of a musical called *Phantom of the Opera*. It changed her life. She suddenly knew what she wanted to be when she grew up. She wanted to be an opera singer. She asked her parents if she could start taking singing lessons. They said yes.

But some other people told Rubin that she could never be an opera singer. Why? Because she had been born blind. Those people said nobody would hire an opera singer who was blind. How could she learn the music? How could she move around on the stage during a performance without bumping into things or falling into the orchestra pit?

But Rubin proved them wrong. Today, she sings on opera stages around the world. She memorizes music by listening to the notes over and over again. She also memorizes where she needs to be on the stage during a performance.

80
Students who attend Laurie Rubin's performing arts school each year

- The school, Ohana Arts, is located near Rubin's home in Hawaii.
- It is for children who are blind and children who are sighted.
- Rubin started the school because she wants to help children who dream of becoming musicians.

Rubin wants children to know that they should never be afraid to follow their dreams.

IN THE MIDDLE

Rubin is a mezzo-soprano. That is the second-highest type of voice a woman opera singer can have. The highest type of voice is called soprano. The lowest is called contralto.

Yu Xiuhua: Sharing Her Life Through Poetry

Yu Xiuhua in 2015.

Yu Xiuhua was born in 1976 in a small village in China. Her parents were poor farmers, and she was their only child. She tried to help her parents on the farm, but she could do only simple chores, such as feeding fresh grass to the family's rabbits. That's because Yu was born with cerebral palsy. It's a condition that affects the body's muscles. Yu has difficulty controlling the muscles in her arms and legs.

Even with her family around her, Yu felt very alone. Then, when she was 27, she decided to write a poem. She wanted to put her feelings down on paper. She chose poetry because it uses fewer words than other kinds of writing. Fewer words meant less time trying to keep the muscles in her hand steady as she held a pen or typed on a computer.

Writing poems helped Yu feel less lonely, so she kept doing it. But she didn't show her poems to anybody for about 10 years. One day, however, she decided to post one of her poems on her blog. It was a sensation. People wanted to read more of her poems.

Within a year, Yu had become one of China's best-known poets. She has published several books of her poetry. She has also traveled around the world to talk about her life and her writing.

2,000
Poems Yu Xiuhua wrote before she started sharing them with others

- Many of her poems are about living on a farm in a small Chinese village.
- Yu writes in Chinese, but her poems have been translated into many languages.
- Musicians have turned some of her poems into songs.

THINK ABOUT IT

Poets often write about where they live. If you were going to write a poem, what would you write about?

Gilles Tréhin: Creating an Imaginary City

Gilles Tréhin with his partner Catherine.

Gilles Tréhin was born in France in 1972. He has autism spectrum disorder. His brain developed in a way that makes him see, hear, and feel the world differently than other people. As a result, some things are difficult for him to do. In particular, he finds it hard to talk with other people. That's because he doesn't always understand what they are feeling when he is talking with them.

Although some activities are difficult for Tréhin, others are remarkably easy. He has always been an amazing artist. When he was a small boy growing up in France, he made detailed drawings of the world around him. Tall skyscrapers and airplanes especially fascinated him. He made many drawings of them. He also started to build a city with towering buildings and an airport out of LEGO bricks.

But soon that city got too big. It took up all the space in Tréhin's bedroom. That's when he realized that he could "build" a better city on paper—by making drawings of it.

Tréhin has been creating his imaginary city ever since. He calls it Urville. He has made hundreds of drawings of the city's streets

11,820,257
People who live in Gilles Tréhin's imaginary city of Urville

- Tréhin has placed the city on an island off the south of France.
- The city has 36 different neighborhoods.
- If Urville were real, it would be the biggest city in Europe.

and buildings. He sketches each drawing first in pencil. Then he uses a pen to fill in all the details.

Urville has a large airport and many skyscrapers. It also has universities and hundreds of shops, restaurants, museums, theaters, churches, and parks. Tréhin has written a detailed imaginary history of the city. He has published all this information and many of the drawings in a book called *Urville*.

URVILLE

GILLES TRÉHIN

Foreword by Uta Frith

Adrian Anantawan: Mastering the Violin Single-Handedly

Adrian Anantawan remembers the day in his Canadian school when all the students were given a musical instrument called a recorder to play. Anantawan didn't know what to do with it. He didn't have enough fingers to cover all the holes. Anantawan had been born without a right hand.

1698
Year when Adrian Anantawan's violin was made

- That makes Anantawan's violin more than 300 years old.
- It was made by a famous Italian family of violin makers whose last name was Amati.
- The Amati family invented the shape of the modern violin.

His parents tried to find other ways he could be a musician. They gave him a trumpet. But it was too loud. They gave him singing lessons. But he didn't really like to sing. Then they gave him a violin.

It wasn't just any violin. Anantawan's parents had a special device built so the

Adrian Anantawan in 2012.

THINK ABOUT IT

Music can help people communicate who they are and what they are feeling. Has music ever helped you express your feelings?

violin's bow could be strapped to the stunted end of his right arm. He could then make the bow move over the violin's strings by pushing it with his right elbow.

Anantawan loved playing the violin. He became very, very good at it. He has played the violin for audiences around the world. He has given special performances at the White House and at the Opening Ceremonies for the 2010 Winter Olympics in Vancouver.

Anantawan was bullied in school because of his missing hand. He sometimes felt as if he didn't belong anywhere. Playing the violin changed that. Through music, he was able to express his feelings. He says people

Anantawan performing with the Boston Landmarks Orchestra in 2016.

were then able to see him for what was in his heart, not what was missing from his arm.

19

Frida Kahlo: Painting through Her Pain

Frida Kahlo was born in 1907 in a village near Mexico City. When she was six years old, she got a

Frida Kahlo in 1944.

disease called polio. It caused her muscles to weaken. Kahlo recovered from the illness. But afterward, her right leg was always shorter and thinner than her left one. She limped when she walked.

Kahlo was very interested in science. She wanted to become a doctor. When she was 18, she was seriously injured in a bus accident. She broke her spine, and a steel handrail pierced her body. She had to stay in bed for many weeks. To pass the time, she started to paint portraits of herself and her friends.

Kahlo was eventually able to walk again. But the pain of her injuries never went away. She had to give up her dream of becoming a doctor. Soon, though, she had a new dream. She wanted to become an artist.

Kahlo became one of Mexico's greatest artists. Her paintings are in museums around the world. They have bold and vibrant colors. They also contain many Mexican symbols and animals. Kahlo married another famous Mexican artist, Diego Rivera. She died in Mexico in 1954, just a few days after her 47th birthday.

Kahlo with artist and husband, Diego Rivera, and a self-portrait from 1933 (right).

143
Paintings Frida Kahlo completed during her lifetime

- Kahlo painted herself 55 times.
- She said she painted herself so often because she knew herself best.
- She often expressed her pain in her self-portraits.

MIXING REAL WITH MAGIC

Some people use the term "magic realism" to describe Kahlo's work. Magic realism is a style of painting. The artist paints strange things into ordinary settings. That makes the painting look both realistic and magical. Magic realism was particularly popular among artists early in the 20th century.

Antoine Hunter: Connecting through Dance

could see how much fun it was to dance. He asked his mother if he could take dance lessons. She said no. She didn't have enough money to pay for the lessons.

Hunter got his first chance to take dance lessons in high school. His school offered a free dance class as part of its physical education program. Hunter loved the class. He had often felt alone and bullied at school, mainly because his deafness made it difficult for him to communicate with other students. But when he was dancing, he felt he was finally "speaking" a language that everybody understood.

Dancing changed Hunter's life. He went on to learn many different types of dance, including ballet, jazz, hip-hop, African dance, and even belly dancing. He dances to the music by feeling its vibrations.

When he was five years old, Antoine Hunter saw the *Nutcracker* ballet near his home in Oakland, California. He couldn't hear the music because he is deaf. But he

Hunter performs for the Urban Jazz Dance Company.

Hunter has performed with dance groups around the world. And he has his own dance troupe in San Francisco, where he now lives. He says being a dancer is like being a wizard. It's a way of creating magical moments—and connecting with other people.

TALKING WITHOUT SPEAKING

People who are deaf often use sign language when "talking" with each other. Sign language is a mixture of hand signs, body movements, facial expressions, and mouth actions. As with spoken languages, people use different sign languages in different parts of the world.

2013

Year when Antoine Hunter started the International Deaf Dance Festival

- The festival is held every year in San Francisco.
- It brings together dancers who are deaf from around the world.
- One of the festival's goals is to inspire people of all hearing abilities to be creative.

23

Yinka Shonibare: Following His Dream

Yinka Shonibare in 2016.

Yinka Shonibare always wanted to be an artist. While growing up in Great Britain and Nigeria, he took many art classes. He learned how to paint and to sculpt things out of wood, clay, and other materials. Shonibare also loved to read. Through books, he was able to imagine himself having magical adventures around the world.

When Shonibare was a teenager, he went to a special school in London to study art. One day, he got very sick. He had a rare illness. His spinal cord had become swollen. He couldn't move any muscles in his arms or legs.

Shonibare stayed in a hospital for many months. Eventually he got better, although one side of his body stayed paralyzed.

But he didn't give up his dream of becoming an artist. Shonibare returned to art school. He started making sculptures out of the brightly colored fabric worn by many people in Africa.

Shonibare's sculptures are now in cities around the world. To build them, he works with a team of helpers. He imagines how the sculptures will look. He makes detailed drawings of them on paper. His helpers then build the sculptures. Shonibare supervises the building from his wheelchair.

11

One sculpture is called *Wind Sculpture VII*. It is in front of the Smithsonian National Museum of African Art in Washington, DC. Although made with steel and fiberglass, it is painted the colors of an African-style fabric. The sculpture stands 20 feet (6 m) tall. It looks like a giant ship's sail, billowing in the wind. It celebrates the culture and history of African Americans.

37

Sails on Yinka Shonibare's sculpture *Nelson's Ship in a Bottle*

- Shonibare made this sculpture in 2010.
- It is a smaller copy of a famous 19th-century British warship.
- The sails are made out of African-style fabric.

Shonibare's sculpture, *Nelson's Ship in a Bottle*, is outside the National Maritime Museum in London, UK.

Octavia Butler: Writing Scary Stories

Octavia Butler was born into an African American family in 1947. She was a shy child. She also had dyslexia. This is a learning problem that makes it hard to read and spell. But Butler loved books. She would go to her local library in Pasadena, California, as often as she could. Finishing a book just took her longer than it did for other kids. She read very slowly.

Butler felt very alone when she was growing up. She didn't have any brothers or sisters, and her classmates were often mean to her. She soon discovered that writing adventure stories about imaginary people and places made her feel better. By the time she was 10 years old, she was carrying a big notebook around with her. She would write in it whenever she had some extra time.

Butler loved to watch scary movies. One day, she watched a science fiction movie on television. She thought the story was silly. She also thought she could write a much better—and scarier—story.

And she did. Butler grew up to become one of America's best-known science fiction writers. She published many books and won

many awards before her death in 2006. Today, her stories continue to be read by people around the world.

Fledgling was the final book Butler published before her death in 2006.

MULTIPLE AWARD-WINNING AUTHOR OF
PARABLE OF THE TALENTS AND *KINDRED*

OCTAVIA E. BUTLER

fledgling

"COMPLETELY TRANSFORMS [VAMPIRE LORE] IN A STARTLINGLY ORIGINAL STORY ABOUT RACE, FAMILY, AND FREE WILL"
WASHINGTON POST

$295,000

Amount Octavia Butler received in 1995 for a MacArthur Fellowship

- This prize is nicknamed the Genius Grant.
- Butler was the first science fiction writer to win it.
- She used the money to write a vampire story.

A MIX OF FACT AND FICTION

Science fiction is a special type of storytelling. The stories are based in real science, but they have wildly imaginative characters and plots. Science fiction stories can be about anything. But many are about aliens from outer space, humanlike robots, or people traveling far into the future.

Learn More: Types of Disability

A disability is any condition of the body or mind that makes it more difficult for a person to do certain activities.

Some people are born with a disability. Other people become disabled after an accident or an illness. Some disabilities are visible. Others aren't.

There are three main types of disabilities:

- A physical disability affects a person's movement. People can become physically disabled after being paralyzed or losing an arm or a leg in an accident. Many medical conditions can also make it difficult to move. An example is cerebral palsy. It makes muscles weak and hard to control.

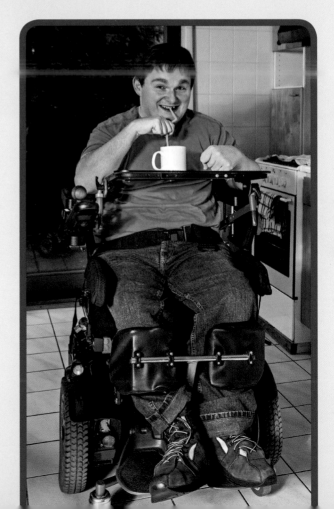

- A sensory disability affects a person's ability to use one or more of the body's five senses. Those senses are sight, hearing, smell, touch, and taste. Blindness and hearing loss are examples of this type of disability.

- A learning disability affects how people learn new things. Dyslexia, which makes it difficult to learn how to read and spell, is an example of this type of disability.

People with disabilities can do many of the same things that other people do. They just do them in a different way.

Glossary

bow
A piece of wood with strands of horsehair that is used to play a stringed instrument, like a violin.

fabric
A piece of cloth.

fiberglass
A type of material that's made from the fine fibers of glass.

orchestra pit
The area in a theater where the musicians play their instruments. It's usually located below the front of the stage.

paralyzed
Not being able to move a part of the body.

realistic
Representing something as it really is; lifelike.

recorder
A musical instrument that looks like a tube with holes.

sculpture
A statue or other work of art that's made by carving or shaping wood, stone, or clay.

sketch
A drawing that's done quickly. It's often later used to make a more finished picture.

skyscraper
A very tall building.

timpani
A large drum.

Read More

Elder, Jennifer. *Different Like Me: My Book of Autism Heroes.* London, PA: Jessica Kingsley Publishers, 2005.

Frith, Margaret. *Frida Kahlo: The Artist Who Painted Herself.* New York: Grosset & Dunlap, 2003.

Helsby, Genevieve, and Evelyn Glennie. *Meet the Instruments of the Orchestra.* Redhill, UK: Naxos Books, 2007.

Index

About the Author

Susan Perry lives in Virginia with her family. She writes about science and health for children and grown-ups. She wants to thank her grandson, Colin, for all his help.

READ MORE FROM 12-STORY LIBRARY

Every 12-Story Library Book is available in many fomats. For more information, visit **12StoryLibrary.com**